Let's go Hunting

with our eyes

by Nancy Streza

Hardcover ISBN: 978-1-5324-3746-5
Paperback ISBN: 978-1-62395-4-666
eISBN: 9781623952808
Images licensed from Fotolia.com
First Edition
Published in the United States by Xist Publishing
www.xistpublishing.com

xist Publishing

2

Let's go hunting
(with our eyes)

3

I see a beautiful doe -
a female deer

and a buck with
his antlers

and their fawn over here.

7

This female elk is called a cow

If we see a bull elk,
we'll just say, "WOW!"

We'll look for a
reindeer—
called a "caribou"

and a bushy-tailed fox

and her little cub, too.

There's a sneaky coyote

17

and a gigantic moose.

19

Do you see that eagle...

the turkey...

the goose?

Errrch!! There's a
smelly skunk

24

and a
frightening boar

a scary-looking wolf!

Oh, let's hunt for more!

Look at the tail on
that beaver

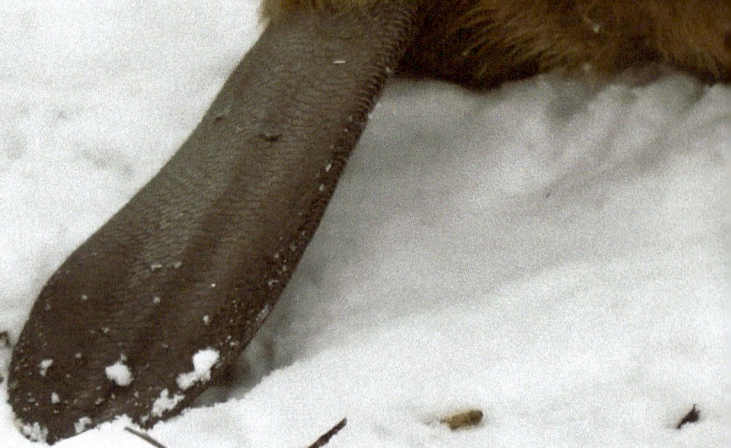

and the size of
that bear!

The horns on that buffalo

and that goat
over there!

36

This kind of hunting

requires no gun.

We hunt with our eyes

Come on! It's fun!

www.ingramcontent.com/pod-product-compliance
Lightning Source LLC
Chambersburg PA
CBHW040418110426

42813CB00013B/2687